Alfred A. Knopf
Random House/Singer School Division
First Voices The third book
edited by Geoffrey Summerfield

First Voices The third book

edited by Geoffrey Summerfield

ALFRED A. KNOPF
Alfred A. Knopf, Inc.
New York

RANDOM HOUSE/SINGER SCHOOL DIVISION
Random House, Inc.
New York • Brandon, Miss. • Dallas • Atlanta • Los Altos

Library of Congress Catalog Card Number: 74-148381
Standard Book Numbers: 394-02405-2 (School edition)
                       92301-4 (Gibraltar edition)

Manufactured in the United States of America
First American Edition

Cover design by Alan Spain

Contents

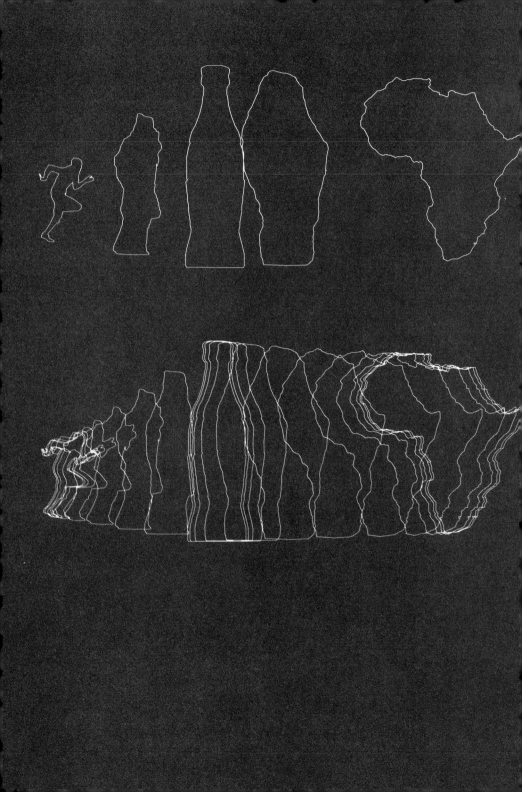

A View of Things

what I love about dormice is their size
what I hate about rain is its sneer
flag what I love about the Bratach Gorm is its unflappability
what I hate about scent is its smell
what I love about newspapers is their etaoin shrdl
what I hate about philosophy is its pursed lip
what I love about Rory is his old grouse
what I hate about Pam is her pinkie
what I love about semi-precious stones is their preciousness
what I hate about diamonds is their mink
what I love about poetry is its ion engine
bristles what I hate about hogs is their setae
what I love about love is its porridge-spoon
what I hate about hate is its eyes
what I love about hate is its salts
what I hate about love is its dog
what I love about Hank is his string vest
what I hate about the twins is their three gloves
what I love about Mabel is her teeter
what I hate about gooseberries is their look, feel, smell, and taste
what I love about the world is its shape
what I hate about a gun is its lock, stock, and barrel
what I love about bacon-and-eggs is its predictability
what I hate about derelict buildings is their reluctance to
    disintegrate
what I love about a cloud is its unpredictability
what I hate about you, chum, is your china
what I love about many waters is their inability to quench love

EDWIN MORGAN

Six Riddles

1 I can throw an egg against the wall,
   And it will neither break nor fall.

2 There was a girl in our town,
   Silk an' satin was her gown,
   Silk an' satin, gold an' velvet;
   Guess her name, three times I've telled it.

3 Can you tell me why
   A hypocrite's eye
   Can better descry
   Than you or I
   On how many toes
   A pussycat goes?

4 On the hill sits a green house,
   In the green house is a white house,
   In the white house is a red house,
   In the red house are a lot of little black and white men.

5 Old Mother Twitchett, she had but one eye,
   And a great long tail that she let fly;
   And every time she went through a gap,
   She left a bit of her tail in the trap.

6 Spell mousetrap in three letters.
   Spell dried grass in three letters.
   Spell hard water in three letters.
   Spell donkey in three letters.

TRADITIONAL AMERICAN

Decapitations

Behead a loud
call   and find a
plaything

Behead a stream of
water   and find
a bird

Behead a fish
and find an army
in flight

Behead a weapon
and find a
fruit

Behead a month
and find a
beautiful form

Behead a strong
wind   and find you
are not the first

Behead a country in
Europe   and find
suffering.

'C.C.'

Pl. XX

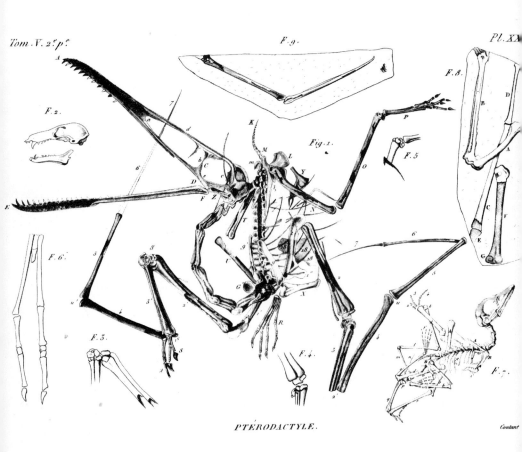

F. 9.

F. 8.

F. 2.

Fig. 1.

F. 5.

K

F. 6.

F. 3.

F. 4.

F. 7.

PTÉRODACTYLE.

Coulant

Kingley Bottom

covered in creepers Beneath these bine-looped yew-boughs
    Gorse blossom is outspread
Like gold that lies unguarded
    By dragons that hang dead.

All but one pterodactyl
    That hid in mist and rain
High over Kingley Bottom
    Hums like an aeroplane.

ANDREW YOUNG

The Toaster

A silver-scaled Dragon with jaws flaming red
Sits at my elbow and toasts my bread.
I hand him fat slices, and then, one by one,
He hands them back when he sees they are done.

WILLIAM JAY SMITH

Horses

A young lad and an old man,
The ebb and flow of life,
Stepping out together.
'Horses, Gran'pa, will the
Horses be there today?'
'Ay lad! Today, yesterday and tomorrow,
The horses will be there.'
'Tell me again how they will look, Gran'pa.'
'How they will look, boy?
Well, today they will have caught
The spirit of the wind.
They will prance and leap and race.
Over the rocks they will gallop, heads
Held high with tossing manes.
White horses, lad! Fiery! Strong!

They will race to meet us, with foam
At their nostrils.
And we will hear them come,
Feel their pounding under our feet.
Then they will turn, lad, curl and whirl away.
They'll go back and return again.
Ay, lad! There will be white horses
On the sea today!'

LYNNE WILLIAMS Age 13

The Sharks

Well, then, the last day the sharks appeared.
Dark fins appear, innocent
as if in fair warning. The sea becomes
sinister, are they everywhere?
I tell you, they break six feet of water.
Isn't it the same sea, and won't we
play in it any more?
I liked it clear and not
too calm, enough waves
to fly in on. For the first time
I dared to swim out of my depth.
It was sundown when they came, the time
when a sheen of copper stills the sea,
not dark enough for moonlight, clear enough
to see them easily. Dark
the sharp lift of the fins.

DENISE LEVERTOV

Rattlesnake Ceremony Song

The king snake said to the rattlesnake:
Do not touch me!
You can do nothing with me.
Lying with your belly full,
Rattlesnake of the rock pile,
Do not touch me!
There is nothing you can do,
You rattlesnake with your belly full,
Lying where the ground squirrel holes are thick.
Do not touch me!
What can you do to me?
Rattlesnake in the tree clump,
Stretched in the shade,
You can do nothing;
Do not touch me!
Rattlesnake of the plains,
You whose white eye
The sun shines on,
Do not touch me!

TRADITIONAL
North American Indian poem translated from the Yokuts by A. L. Kroeber

A Withered Tree

Not a twig or a leaf on the old tree,
Wind and frost harm it no more.
A man could pass through the hole in its belly,
Ants crawl searching under its peeling bark.
Its only lodger, the toadstool which dies in a morning,
The birds no longer visit in the twilight.
But its wood can still spark tinder.
It does not care yet to be only the void at its heart.

HAN YU Chinese poem translated by A.C. Graham

Starry Snail

You crept out after the rain
After the starry rain

The stars have built a small house for you
By themselves out of your bones
Where are you taking it on that towel

Time goes limping after you
To catch you up to trample you
Put out your horns snail

You slide over the vast countenance
Which you will never be able to see
Straight to the jaws of the good-for-nothing

Turn on to the life line
Of my dreaming palm
Before it is too late

And leave me as a legacy
The miraculous towel of silver

VASKO POPA
Yugoslavian poem translated from the Serbo-Croatian by Anne Pennington

The Snail's Monologue

Shall I dwell in my shell?
Shall I not dwell in my shell?
Dwell in shell?
Rather not dwell?
Shall I not dwell,
shall I dwell,
dwell in shell,
shall I shell,
shallIshellIshallIshellIshallI . . . ?

(The snail gets so entangled with his thoughts or, rather, the
thoughts run away with him so that he must postpone the
decision.)

CHRISTIAN MORGENSTERN German poem translated by Max Knight

The Locust

What is a locust?
Its head, a grain of corn; its neck, the hinge of a knife;
Its horns, a bit of thread; its chest is smooth and burnished;
Its body is like a knife-handle;
Its hock, a saw; its spittle, ink;
Its underwings, clothing for the dead.
On the ground – it is laying eggs;
In flight – it is like the clouds.
Approaching the ground, it is rain glittering in the sun;
Lighting on a plant, it becomes a pair of scissors;
Walking, it becomes a razor;
Desolation walks with it.

TRADITIONAL
Madagascan poem translated by A. Marre and Willard R. Trask

The Bat

By day the bat is cousin to the mouse.
He likes the attic of an ageing house.

His fingers make a hat about his head.
His pulse beat is so slow we think him dead.

He loops in crazy figures half the night
Among the trees that face the corner light.

But when he brushes up against a screen,
We are afraid of what our eyes have seen:

For something is amiss or out of place
When mice with wings can wear a human face.

THEODORE ROETHKE

Haiku

A bitter morning:
  sparrows sitting together
    without any necks.

J.W. HACKETT

Remember the chameleon

Remember the chameleon. He was a well-behaved chameleon and nothing could be brought against his record. As a chameleon he had done the things that should have been done and left undone the things that should have been left undone. He was a first-class unimpeachable chameleon and nobody had anything on him. But he came to a Scotch plaid and tried to cross it. In order to cross he had to imitate six different yarn colors, first one and then another and back to the first or second. He was a brave chameleon and died at the crossroads true to his chameleon instincts.

CARL SANDBURG

The Frog

What a wonderful bird the frog are –
When he sit, he stand almost;
When he hop, he fly almost.
He ain't got no sense hardly;
He ain't got no tail hardly either.
When he sit, he sit on what he ain't got – almost.

ANONYMOUS

French Persian Cats Having a Ball

chat
shah shah
    chat
        chat shah cha ha
        shah chat cha ha
   shah
   chat
cha
cha

            ha
            chat
            chat
         chatshahchat
      chachacha   chachacha
        shahchatshah
           shah
           shah
             ha

cha
cha
chatcha
   cha
  shahcha
     cha
    chatcha
       cha
      shahcha
        cha
        cha

               sh   ch
              aha
              ch   sh

EDWIN MORGAN

HIERONIMVS BOS INVÉ. F.

Elephants are Different to Different People

Wilson and Pilcer and Snack stood before the zoo elephant.

Wilson said, 'What is its name? Is it from Asia or Africa? Who feeds it? Is it a he or a she? How old is it? Do they have twins? How much does it cost to feed? How much does it weigh? If it dies, how much will another one cost? If it dies, what will they use the bones, the fat, and the hide for? What use is it besides to look at?'

Pilcer didn't have any questions; he was murmuring to himself, 'It's a house by itself, walls and windows, the ears came from tall cornfields, by God; the architect of those legs was a workman, by God; he stands like a bridge out across deep water; the face is sad and the eyes are kind; I know elephants are good to babies.'

Snack looked up and down and at last said to himself, 'He's a tough son of a gun outside and I'll bet he's got a strong heart, I'll bet he's strong as a copper-riveted boiler inside.'

They didn't put up any arguments.

They didn't throw anything in each other's faces.

Three men saw the elephant three ways

And let it go at that.

They didn't spoil a sunny Sunday afternoon;

'Sunday comes only once a week,' they told each other.

CARL SANDBURG

Earthy Anecdote

Every time the bucks went clattering
Over Oklahoma
A firecat bristled in the way.

Wherever they went,
They went clattering,
Until they swerved
In a swift, circular line
To the right,
Because of the firecat.

Or until they swerved
In a swift, circular line
To the left,
Because of the firecat.

The bucks clattered.
The firecat went leaping,
To the right, to the left,
And
Bristled in the way.

Later, the firecat closed his bright eyes
And slept.

WALLACE STEVENS

Indomitable

The chickadee the cat clawed
Is here this morning on one leg.
With no tailfeathers left he lights
And, balancing, begins to beg.

MARK VAN DOREN

Upstairs

I went upstairs
to watch it move.
I kept it there
under some clothes
in a small box.
It felt so warm
when I held it.
Then I dropped it.
It didn't move
for a long time.
And the next day
when I touched it,
it felt funny.
It wouldn't crawl.
It wasn't warm.
Something was bad
inside. I knew
it wasn't mine
the way it was.
It's still up there.
I don't want it
because it's cold.
I won't go near.
I stay downstairs.
It's warm down here
and I'm happy.

JOHN STEVENS WADE

The Dead Butterfly

1   Now I see its whiteness
is not white but green, traced with green,
and resembles the stones
of which the city is built,
quarried high in the mountains.

2   Everywhere among the marigolds
the rainblown roses and the hedges
evergreen shrub of tamarisk are white
butterflies this morning, in constant
tremulous movement, only those
that lie dead revealing
their rockgreen color and the bold
cut of the wings.

DENISE LEVERTOV

from Briggflatts

I am neither snake nor lizard,
I am the slowworm.

Ripe wheat is my lodging. I polish
my side on pillars of its transept,
gleam in its occasional light.
Its swaying
copies my gait.

Vaults stored with slugs to relish,
my quilt a litter of husks, I prosper
lying low, little concerned.
My eyes sharpen
when I blink.

Good luck to reaper and miller!
Grubs adhere even to stubble.
Come plowtime
the ditch is near.

Sycamore seed twirling,
O, writhe to its measure!
Dust swirling scans pleasure.

Thorns prance in a gale.
In air snow flickers,
twigs tap,
elms drip.

Swaggering, shimmering fall,
drench and towel us all!

BASIL BUNTING

The Garden Hose

In the gray evening
I see a long green serpent
With its tail in the dahlias.

It lies in loops across the grass
And drinks softly at the faucet.

I can hear it swallow.

BEATRICE JANOSCO

Haiku

Rain drums on the pane
    and runs down, wavering the world
        into a dream.

J.W. HACKETT

Orgy

```
c a n t e r c a n t e r c a n t e r c a n t e r
a n t e a t e r a n t e a t e r a n t e a t e r
a n t e n c o u n t e r a n t e n c o u n t e r
a n t e n n a r e a c t a n t e n n a r e a c t
a n t a n t a n t a n t a n t a n t a n t a n t
a n t a n t a n t a n t a n t a n t a n t a n t
a n t a n t a n t a n t a n t a n t a n t a n t
a n t a n t a n t a n t a n t a n t a n t a n t
c a n t c o u n t a n t c a n t c o u n t a n t
a n a c c o u n t a n t a n a c c o u n t a n t
a n t e a t e r a n t e a t e r a n t e a t e r
e a t e a t e a t e a t e a t e a t e a t e a t
e a t e a t e a t e a t e a t e a t e a t e a t
a n t e a t e n a n t e a t e n a n t e a t e n
n e c t a r n e c t a r n e c t a r n e c t a r
t r a n c e t r a n c e t r a n c e t r a n c e
 *   *   *   *   *   *   *   *   *   *   *   *   *   *
c a n t e a t a n a n t c a n t e a t a n a n t
a n t e a t e r c a n t a n t e a t e r c a n t
n o t a n a n t n o t a n a n t n o t a n a n t
 *   *   *   *   *   *   *   *   *   *   *   *   *   *
t r a n c e t r a n c e t r a n c e t r a n c e
o c o n t e n t o c o n t e n t o c o n t e n t
n o c a n t e r n o c a n t e r n o c a n t e r
```

EDWIN MORGAN

The Sea Serpent Chantey

1 There's a snake on the western wave
And his crest is red.
He is long as a city street,
And he eats the dead.
There's a hole in the bottom of the sea
Where the snake goes down.
And he waits in the bottom of the sea
For the men that drown.

Let the audience join in the chorus

    This is the voice of the sand
    (The sailors understand)
    'There is far more sea than sand,
    There is far more sea than land.
        Yo . . . ho, yo . . . ho.'

2 He waits by the door of his cave
While the ages moan.
He cracks the ribs of the ships
With his teeth of stone.
In his gizzard deep and long
Much treasure lies.
Oh, the pearls and the Spanish gold . . .
And the idols' eyes . . .
Oh, the totem poles . . . the skulls . . .
The altars cold . . .
The wedding rings, the dice. . .
The buoy bells old.

    This is the voice of the sand
    (The sailors understand)
    'There is far more sea than sand,
    There is far more sea than land.
        Yo . . . ho, yo . . . ho.'

3 Dive, mermaids, with sharp swords
And cut him through,
And bring us the idols' eyes
And the red gold too.
Lower the grappling hooks
Good pirate men

And drag him up by the tongue
From his deep wet den.

Repeat as a
second chorus
many times
   We will sail to the end of the world,
   We will nail his hide
    To the mainmast of the moon
    In the evening tide.

4   Or will you let him live,
The deep-sea thing,
With the wrecks of all the world
In a black wide ring
By the hole in the bottom of the sea
Where the snake goes down,
Where he waits in the bottom of the sea
For the men that drown?
    This is the voice of the sand
    (The sailors understand)
    'There is far more sea than sand,
    There is far more sea than land.
      Yo . . . ho, yo . . . ho.'

VACHEL LINDSAY

Dunce Song No. 4

Then I'll be four-footed,
And modest with fur.
All over, all under,
Seemly and still.

Then I'll be patient:
A part of the ground.
I will go slowly,
And lowly – oh, sweet,

Then I'll be one of them
He that made all
Looks after the longest,
And tenderest loves.

Then I'll be quiet –
You can be quick –
And lie down all summer,
All winter, and sleep.

(This dunce believes what no intelligent person can believe,
that he might become an animal. I'm sure it's a very deep
desire in every human being to be an animal. We can't. We're
not animals and never were, but many of us long to be. The
chief basis for our longing is the desire to sleep as much as
animals do. Every human being caught taking a nap is
ashamed. No animal is. That's just one of the advantages of
being an animal. Another advantage is that he has hair all
over him.)

MARK VAN DOREN

Natural Song (Riddle)

Stood wooden wiggled in earth way under
A toenail scraped a mammoth's tusk
Jounced and jittered all these lippy leaves

MAY SWENSON

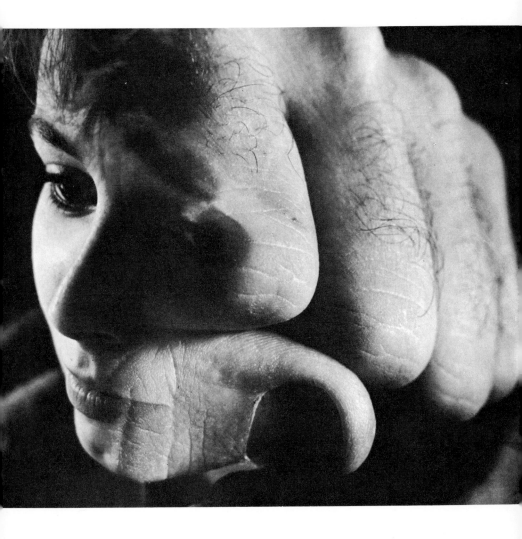

Micky Thumps

As I was going down Treak Street
molasses For half a pound of treacle,
Who should I meet but my old friend Micky Thumps?
merry-making He said to me, 'Wilt thou come to our wake?'
 I thought a bit,
 I thought a bit,
 I said I didn't mind:
 So I went.

As I was sitting on our doorstep
Who should come by but my old friend Micky Thumps'
  brother?
He said to me, 'Wilt thou come to our house?
Micky is ill.'
 I thought a bit,
 I thought a bit,
 I said I didn't mind:
 So I went.

And he were ill.
very He were gradely ill.
He said to me,
'Wilt thou come to my funeral, mon, if I die?'
 I thought a bit,
 I thought a bit,
 I said I didn't mind:
 So I went.

And it were a funeral.
Some stamped on his grave:
Some spat on his grave:
But I scraped my eyes out for my old friend Micky Thumps.

ANONYMOUS

Step on a Crack

Step on a crack,
You'll break your mother's back;
Step on a line,
You'll break your father's spine.

Step in a ditch,
Your mother's nose will itch;
Step in the dirt,
You'll tear your father's shirt.

TRADITIONAL AMERICAN

Be Merry

Whenever you see the hearse go by
And think to yourself that you're gonna die,
Be merry, my friends, be merry.

They put you in a big white shirt
And cover you over with tons of dirt,
Be merry, my friends, be merry.

They put you in a long-shaped box
And cover you over with tons of rocks,
Be merry, my friends, be merry.

The worms crawl out and the worms crawl in,
The ones that crawl in are lean and thin,
The ones that crawl out are fat and stout,
Be merry, my friends, be merry.

Your eyes fall in and your hair falls out
And your brains come tumbling down your snout,
Be merry, my friends, be merry.

TRADITIONAL ENGLISH

Still Here

I've been scarred and battered.
My hopes the wind done scattered.
Snow has friz me, sun has baked me.
   Looks like between 'em
   They done tried to make me
Stop laughin', stop lovin', stop livin' –
   But I don't care!
   I'm still here!

LANGSTON HUGHES

Fairy Tale

He built himself a house,
   his foundations,
   his stones,
   his walls,
   his roof overhead,
   his chimney and smoke,
   his view from the window.

He made himself a garden,
   his fence,
   his thyme,
   his earthworm,
   his evening dew.

He cut out his bit of sky above.

And he wrapped the garden in the sky
and the house in the garden
and packed the lot in a handkerchief

and went off
lone as an arctic fox
through the cold
unending
rain
into the world.

MIROSLAV HOLUB Czechoslovakian poem translated by Ian Milner

Mips and ma the mooly moo

Mips and ma the mooly moo,
The likes of him is biting who,
A cow's a care and who's a coo? –
What footie does is final.

My dearest dear my fairest fair,
Your father tossed a cat in air,
Though neither you nor I was there, –
What footie does is final.

Be large as an owl, be slick as a frog,
Be good as a goose, be big as a dog,
Be sleek as a heifer, be long as a hog, –
What footie will do will be final.

THEODORE ROETHKE

What's inside the moon?

What's inside the moon?
   There's hot water inside.
What's the sky made of?
   It was made out of white snow.
If you cut the sun open what would you see?
   Terrible looking enemies.
When you write you look at your words. Have you thought of
     cutting them open to see what's inside?
   No. But if a person was crazy the answer would be yes.
What's inside colors?
   There's pink stars.
Where is the end of the universe?
   In back of the swimming pools.
How old is adventure?
   It is sixty thousand years old.
Which color is older, black or white?
   Black because you can outline me.

QUESTIONS BY VIVIAN TUFT Age 9
ANSWERS BY FONTESSA MOORE Age 9

Sometimes when I talk

Sometimes when I talk
nobody answers me.
I feel as if they're deaf
when they really aren't.
I feel like shouting
in their ear
but I mind my manners.
I ask again
they say 'Yes, yes,'
but nothing
more.
I feel like
walking away
but I stay.
I give up asking
and walk
away.

JANE HORVITZ Age 9

On Making Tea

The water bubbles
Should become happy;
Not angry.

The tea leaves
Should become excited;
But not violently so.

The pouring of the water
On the leaves
Should be a conception;
Not a confusion.

The union of the tea and water
Should be allowed to dream;
But not to sleep.

Now follow some moments of rest.

The tea is then gently poured
Into simple, clean containers,
And served before smiling
And understanding friends.

R.L. WILSON

Sink Song

Scouring out the porridge pot,
  Round and round and round!

Out with all the scraith and scoopery,
Lift the eely ooly droopery,
Chase the glubbery slubbery gloopery
  Round and round and round!

Out with all the doleful dithery,
Ladle out the slimy slithery,
Hunt and catch the hithery thithery,
  Round and round and round!

Out with all the obbly gubbly,
On the stove it burns so bubbly,
Use the spoon and use it doubly,
　　Round and round and round!

J.A. LINDON

The Song of the Bottle

Let us sing the song of the bottle, aaa!
Its belly is clear like water,
But you can't see its heart.
Its mouth is on the top of its head, aaa!
Listen, listen, o men!
To lift it, you take it by the neck.
Its fathers laid on it a nasty curse;
You cannot knock one against another,
For their bellies would be cut
To punish them.
Who touches their wounds
Will be torn by a sharp tooth.
When put in water, a bottle breathes quickly,
Like a drowning man.
The white men fill it with rum
Up to its shoulders
And then bring it to us.
This is the song of the bottle, aaa!

TRADITIONAL Madagascan poem translated by A. Fiedler

accidentally

accidentally
broke a teacup –
reminds me
how good it feels
to break things

ISHIKAWA TAKUBOKU Japanese poem translated by Carl Sesar

Squishy Words

(to be said when wet)

SQUIFF
SQUIDGE
SQUAMOUS
SQUINNY
SQUELCH
SQUASH
SQUEEGEE
SQUIRT
SQUAB

ALASTAIR REID

Sounds

PLOO is breaking your shoelace.

MRRAAOWL
is what
cats
really say.

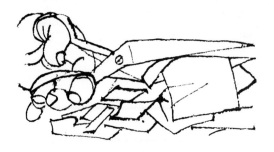

TRIS-TRAS
is scissors cutting paper.

KINCLUNK is a car
going over a manhole cover.

CROOMB is what pigeons
murmur to themselves.

PHLOOPH is sitting
suddenly on a cushion.

 NYO-NYO is speaking with your mouth full.

HARROWOLLOWORRAH is yawning.

PALOOP is the tap dripping in the bath.

RAM TAM GEE PICKAGEE
is
feeling good.

ALASTAIR REID

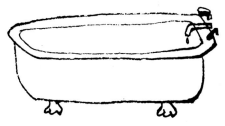

Uncle Jack and the Other Man

I know a man who works on the land
Has a barrel for a chest and a huge flat hand
Can hurl a wheat bag over a fence.

I like to watch him working in the sun
And see the little drops of perspiration run
Like bright flies slowly down his arms.

There was a story once that he took
A tight grip of the London phone book
And pulled it in half – but I don't believe it

Because he *never* boasts – it was Bongo Grass
Who invented that story, he's the worst in class
For pranks and fibs and exaggerations.

But he's certainly strong, and a little strange too:
When you pass him by he hardly speaks to you,
But pats his dogs or makes a cigarette.

He takes no interest in a conversation.
Not like my Uncle Jack. He works at the station
And is always talking when he finds a chance.

If you pay him a visit in his room at night
He'll build up the fire and in the leaping light
He'll tell you stories of ghosts and devils.

Sometimes I stay for hours.
                Uncle Jack
Has skinny white legs and a painful back:
He can't lift a bag or tear the phone book

And yet, he's always interesting. I suppose
I'd like to be like Uncle Jack because he knows
So much . . . but I'd also like to grow – so I can
Hurl things about like that other man.

KEITH HARRISON

A Canner

A canner exceedingly canny,
One morning remarked to his granny,
'A canner can can
Anything that he can,
But a canner can't can a can, can he?'

TRADITIONAL AMERICAN

Suburb

If a naturalist came to this hillside,
he'd find many old newspapers among the weeds
to study.

CHARLES REZNIKOFF

About an excavation

About an excavation
a flock of bright red lanterns
has settled.

CHARLES REZNIKOFF

Among the heaps

Among the heaps of bricks and plaster lies
a girder, still itself among the rubbish.

CHARLES REZNIKOFF

Haiku

With your fists ablaze
with letters and colored stamps
beautiful mailman.

PAUL GOODMAN

Haiku

Orange and golden
the *New York Times* is blazing
in the village dump.

PAUL GOODMAN

The government said

The government said,
'Right now go over to Sheppey
fix up   and do up the roads.'
And so they came,
and put up the lights
which shone through the window
all through the night.
Then they dug up the footings
and laid down the pipes.
Then they laid down the roads
trucks   and now the lorries come whistling
along with their loads.

JULIE DEWBERRY

The concrete highways

The concrete highways crack under the incessant tyres of
two-ton, ten-ton trucks – and the concrete mixers come
with laughing bellies filled with gravel for the repair jobs.

CARL SANDBURG

This smoky winter morning

This smoky winter morning –
do not despise the green jewel shining among the twigs
because it is a traffic light.

CHARLES REZNIKOFF

Haiku

Flashing neon night
   blurred through a steamy window:
      a concert of colors!

J.W. HACKETT

Permit me to warn you

Permit me to warn you
against this automobile rushing to embrace you
with outstretched fender.

CHARLES REZNIKOFF

Arithmetic

Arithmetic is where numbers fly like pigeons in and out of
your head.
Arithmetic tells you how many you lose or win if you know
how many you had before you lost or won.
Arithmetic is seven eleven all good children go to heaven –
or five six bundle of sticks.
Arithmetic is numbers you squeeze from your head to your
hand to your pencil to your paper till you get the answer.
Arithmetic is where the answer is right and everything is
nice and you can look out of the window and see the blue
sky – or the answer is wrong and you have to start all over
again and try again and see how it comes out this time.
If you take a number and double it and double it again and
then double it a few more times, the number gets bigger
and bigger and goes higher and higher and only arithmetic
can tell you what the number is when you decide to
quit doubling.
Arithmetic is where you have to multiply – and you carry the
multiplication table in your head and hope you won't lose
it.
If you have two animal crackers, one good and one bad,
and you eat one and a striped zebra with streaks all over
him eats the other, how many animal crackers will you
have if somebody offers you five six seven and you say No
no no and you say Nay nay nay and you say Nix nix nix?
If you ask your mother for one fried egg for breakfast and
she gives you two fried eggs and you eat both of them,
who is better in arithmetic, you or your mother?

CARL SANDBURG

The Annunciation

It could have been the lonesome neighing of the night
   out there under the window
   when the fire dies down.

It could have been the sound of the trumpets of Jericho,
it could have been the voices
   of little hunchbacks singing under the snow,
it could have been an oak speaking to the willows,
and it could have been the writhing of a mockingbird
   under the wing of an owl.
It could have been an archangel's decision,
it could have been the sinister prophecy of a newt.
It could have been the lament of our one and only love.

But the functionary sitting at our table turned to us,
   saying:

Listen: You must listen.
You are expected to listen.
Listen still more enthusiastically,
let's all listen, you listen, he listens,
they listen, enthusiastically,
listen with enthusiasm,
with enthusiasm listen,
li – s – ten,
LI – S – TEN,
LIS – ten LIS –

And so we didn't hear a thing.

MIROSLAV HOLUB Czechoslovakian poem translated by George Theiner

Teacher, teacher

Teacher, teacher, don't be dumb,
Give me back my bubble gum!

Teacher, teacher, I declare,
Tarzan lost his underwear!

Teacher, teacher, don't be mean,
Give me a dime for the coke machine!

TRADITIONAL AMERICAN

What kind of a liar are you?

What kind of a liar are you?
People lie because they don't remember clear what they saw.
People lie because they can't help making a story better than
    it was the way it happened.
People tell 'white lies' so as to be decent to others.
People lie in a pinch, hating to do it, but lying on because
    it might be worse.
And people lie just to be liars for a crooked personal gain.
    What sort of a liar are you?
    Which of these liars are you?

CARL SANDBURG

How? So!

Mean! He was so mean he wouldn't even let his dog drink
from a mirage.

I'm that unlucky that if it rained soup, everybody would have
a spoon and I'd be left with a fork.

'It was so cold where we were in Greece that the candlelight
froze and we couldn't blow it out.'
    'That's nothing. Where we were, the words came out of our
mouths in pieces of ice, and we had to fry them to see what
we were talking about.'

A newly arrived immigrant wanted to visit the outback and asked the first bushman he met how to get there.

'Out back is out west, out in the never-never where the crows fly backwards; it's way out west o'sunset and right back o'beyond; it's away out back o'Bourke in the great open spaces, where men are men and women are few and far between; it's right away out – well, it's away out back, yer can't miss it.'

tin can hung over a fire

The proper way to cook a cockatoo is to put the bird and an axehead into a billy. Boil them until the axehead is soft. The cockatoo is then ready to eat.

TRADITIONAL AUSTRALIAN

just felt like

just felt like
a train ride –
when I got off
there was
no place to go

ISHIKAWA TAKUBOKU Japanese poem translated by Carl Sesar

I don't know where I'm going

I don't know where I'm going but I'm on my way.
I'll knock you so high in the air you'll starve coming down.
All you get from him you can put in your eye.
If the government tried to pay me for what I don't know
    there wouldn't be enough money in all the mints to pay me.
It's a slow burg – I spent a couple of weeks there one day.
If we had a little ham we could have some ham and eggs if we
    had some eggs.
'Why didn't you zigzag your car and miss him?' 'He was
    zigzagging himself and outguessed me.'
'Are you guilty or not guilty?' 'What else have you?'
'Are you guilty or not guilty?' 'I stands mute.'

CARL SANDBURG

54

Bug Words

(to be said when grumpy)

HUMBUG
BUGBEAR
BUGABOO
BUGBANE
LADYBUG
BOGYBUG
BUGSEED

ALASTAIR REID

The Yawn of Yawns

Once upon a time there was a yawn
Not under the palate not under the hat
Not in the mouth not in anything

It was bigger than everything
Bigger than its own bigness

From time to time
Its dull darkness desperate darkness
In desperation would flash here and there
You might think it was stars

Once upon a time there was a yawn
Boring like any yawn
And still it seems it lasts

VASKO POPA
Yugoslavian poem translated from the Serbo-Croatian by Anne Pennington

The Experiment

Once for experiment I bought
A needle of the better sort.

And furthermore a camel old
Though, one must add, extremely bold.

A rich man too was there with me
Together with his L.S.D.

pounds, shillings and pence

The rich man, I need hardly tell,
Went up to Heaven and rang the bell.

Thereat spake Peter: 'It stands writ
That any camel, strong and fit,

Shall pass the needle's eye before
You put a foot across this door!'

Not doubting God's words in the least
I reassured the valiant beast

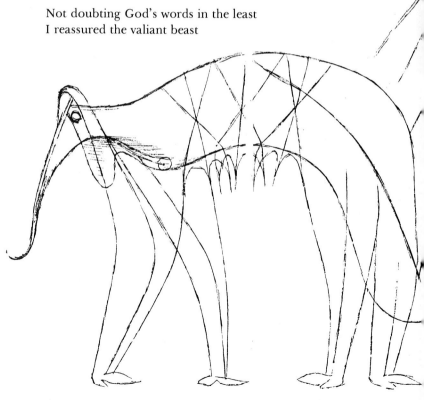

58

Holding behind the needle's eye
A toothsome slice of cherry pie!

And on my oath, the beast went through
– Though creaking cruelly, it is true.

The rich man, who could only blink,
Turned round and muttered: 'Strike me pink!'

CHRISTIAN MORGENSTERN German poem translated by R.F.C. Hull

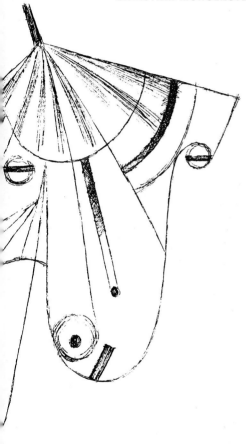

Young Shepherd Bathing his Feet

Only the short, broad, splayed feet
Moved . . .

Feet that had trodden over
Soft soil,
Sand,
open fields Plowed veld,
Mountain rocks
And along narrow tracks,
On Winter clay and
Dust of Summer roads . . .

The short, broad, splayed feet
Moved
In and out . . .

The stumpy toes stretched wide
Apart
And closed together
Then opened wide . . .

In ecstasy.

PETER CLARKE

The Legs

There was this road,
And it led uphill,
And it led downhill,
And round and in and out.

And the traffic was legs,
Legs from the knees down,
Coming and going,
Never pausing.

And the gutters gurgled
With the rain's overflow,
And the sticks on the pavement
Blindly tapped and tapped.

What drew the legs along
Was the never-stopping,
And the senseless, frightening
Fate of being legs.

Legs for the road,
The road for legs,
Resolutely nowhere
In both directions.

My legs at least
Were not in that rout:
On grass by the roadside
Entire I stood,

Watching the unstoppable
Legs go by
With never a stumble
Between step and step.

Though my smile was broad
The legs could not see,
Though my laugh was loud
The legs could not hear.

My head dizzied, then:
I wondered suddenly,
Might I too be a walker
From the knees down?

Gently I touched my shins.
The doubt unchained them:
They had run in twenty puddles
Before I regained them.

ROBERT GRAVES

We are going to see the rabbit

We are going to see the rabbit,
We are going to see the rabbit.
Which rabbit, people say?
Which rabbit, ask the children?
Which rabbit?
The only rabbit,
The only rabbit in England,
Sitting behind a barbed-wire fence
Under the floodlights, neon lights,
Sodium lights,
Nibbling grass
On the only patch of grass
In England, in England
billboards (Except the grass by the hoardings
Which doesn't count.)
We are going to see the rabbit
And we must be there on time.

First we shall go by escalator,
Then we shall go by underground,
highway And then we shall go by motorway
And then by helicopterway,
And the last ten yards we shall have to go
On foot.

And now we are going
All the way to see the rabbit,
We are nearly there,
We are longing to see it,
And so is the crowd
Which is here in thousands
With mounted policemen
And big loudspeakers
And bands and banners,

And everyone has come a long way.
But soon we shall see it
Sitting and nibbling
The blades of grass
On the only patch of grass
In—but something has gone wrong!
Why is everyone so angry,
Why is everyone jostling
And slanging and complaining?

The rabbit has gone,
Yes, the rabbit has gone.
He has actually burrowed down into the earth
And made himself a warren, under the earth,
Despite all these people.
And what shall we do?
What *can* we do?

It is all a pity, you must be disappointed,
Go home and do something else for today,
Go home again, go home for today.
For you cannot hear the rabbit, under the earth,
Remarking rather sadly to himself, by himself,
As he rests in his warren, under the earth:
'It won't be long, they are bound to come,
They are bound to come and find me, even here.'

ALAN BROWNJOHN

64

The Big Nasturtiums

All of a sudden the big nasturtiums
Rose in the night from the ocean's bed,
Rested a while in the light of the morning,
Turning the sand dunes tiger red.

They covered the statue of Abraham Lincoln,
They climbed to the top of our church's spire.
'Grandpa! Grandpa! Come to the window!
Come to the window! Our world's on fire!'

Big nasturtiums in the High Sierras,
Big nasturtiums in the lands below;
Our trains are late and our planes have fallen,
And out in the ocean the whistles blow.

Over the fields and over the forests,
Over the living and over the dead –
'I never expected the big nasturtiums
To come in my lifetime!' Grandpa said.

ROBERT BEVERLY HALE

Moon-Hops

Hops are a menace on the moon, a nuisance crop.
From hilltop to hilltop they hop hopelessly without stop.
Nobody knows what they want to find, they just go on till
   they drop,
Clip-clop at first, then flip-flop, then slip-slop, till finally they
   droopily drop and all their pods pop.

TED HUGHES

Running lightly over spongy ground

Running lightly over spongy ground,
Past the pasture of flat stones,
The three elms,
The sheep strewn on a field,
Over a rickety bridge
Toward the quick-water, wrinkling and rippling.

Hunting along the river,
Down among the rubbish, the bug-riddled foliage,
By the muddy pond-edge, by the bog-holes,
By the shrunken lake, hunting, in the heat of summer.

The shape of a rat?
    It's bigger than that.
    It's less than a leg
    And more than a nose,
    Just under the water
    It usually goes.

Is it soft like a mouse?
Can it wrinkle its nose?
Could it come in the house
On the tips of its toes?

Take the skin of a cat
And the back of an eel,
Then roll them in grease, –
That's the way it would feel.

It's sleek as an otter
With wide webby toes
Just under the water
It usually goes.

THEODORE ROETHKE

The Apple Tree

I was hiding in the crooked apple tree,
Scouting for Indians, when a man came!
I thought it was an Indian, for he
Was running like the wind. There was a flame
Of sunlight on his hand as he drew near,
And then I saw a knife gripped in his fist!

He panted like a horse! His eyes were queer!
Wide-open! Staring frightfully! And, hist!
His mouth stared open like another eye!
And all his hair was matted down with sweat!

I crouched among the leaves lest he should spy
Where I was hiding – so he did not get
His awful eyes on me; but, like the wind,
He fled as if he heard some thing behind!

JAMES STEPHENS

Behind the Hill

Behind the hill I met a man in green.
He asked me if my mother had gone out?
So I said yes. He said I should have seen
The castle where his soldiers sing and shout
From dawn to dark, and told me that he had
A crock of gold inside a hollow tree,
And I could have it. – I wanted money bad
To buy a sword with, and I thought that he
Would keep his solemn word; so, off we went.

He said he had a pound hid in the crock,
And owned the castle too, and paid no rent
To any one, and that you had to knock
Five hundred times. I said, – *Who reckoned up?* –
And he said, – *You insulting little pup!* –

JAMES STEPHENS

Hard Cheese

The grownups are all safe,
Tucked up inside,
Where they belong.

They doze into the telly,
Bustle through the washing-up,
Snore into the fire,
Rustle through the paper.

They're all there,
Out of harm's way.

Now it's *our* street:
All the back yards,
All the gardens,
All the shadows,
All the dark corners,
All the privet-hedges,
All the lampposts,
All the doorways.

Here is an important announcement:
The army of occupation
Is confined to barracks.
Hooray.

We're the natives.
We creep out at night,
Play everywhere,
Swing on *all* the lampposts,
Slit your gizzard?

Then, about nine o'clock,
They send out search parties.

We can hear them coming.
And we crouch
In the garden-sheds,
Behind the dustbins,
Up the alleyways,
Inside the dustbins,
Or stand stock-still,

And pull ourselves in,
As thin as a pin,
Behind the lampposts.

And they stand still,
And peer into the dark.
They take a deep breath –
You can hear it for miles –
And, then, they bawl,
They shout, they caterwaul:
'J-i-i-i-i-mmeeee!'
'Timeforbed. D'youhearme?'
'M-a-a-a-a-reeee!'
'J-o-o-o-o-o-hnneeee!'
'S-a-a-a-a-mmeeee!'
'Mary!' 'Jimmy!'
'Johnny!' 'Sammy!'
Like cats. With very big mouths.

Then we give ourselves up,
Prisoners – of – war.
Till tomorrow night.

But just you wait.
One of these nights
We'll hold out,
We'll lie doggo,
And wait, and wait,
Till they just give up
And mumble
And go to bed.
You just wait.
They'll see!

JUSTIN ST JOHN

The way to the boiler was dark

The way to the boiler was dark,
Dark all the way,
Over slippery cinders
Through the long greenhouse.

The roses kept breathing in the dark.
They had many mouths to breathe with.
My knees made little winds underneath
Where the weeds slept.

There was always a single light
Swinging by the fire pit,
Where the fireman pulled out roses,
glowing bricks   The big roses, the big bloody clinkers.

Once I stayed all night.
The light in the morning came slowly over the white
Snow.
There were many kinds of cool
Air.
Then came steam.

Pipe-knock.

THEODORE ROETHKE

The house-wreckers

The house-wreckers have left the door and a staircase,
now leading to the empty room of night.

CHARLES REZNIKOFF

I know some lonely Houses

I know some lonely Houses off the Road
A Robber'd like the look of –
Wooden barred,
And Windows hanging low,
Inviting to –
A Portico,
Where two could creep –
One – hand the Tools –
The other peep –
To make sure All's Asleep –
Old fashioned eyes –
Not easy to surprise!

How orderly the Kitchen'd look, by night,
With just a Clock –
But they could gag the Tick –
And Mice won't bark –
And so the Walls – don't tell –
None – will –

A pair of Spectacles ajar just stir –
An Almanac's aware –
Was it the Mat – winked,
Or a Nervous Star?
The Moon – slides down the stair,
To see who's there!

There's plunder – where –
Tankard, or Spoon –
Earring – or Stone –
A Watch – Some Ancient Brooch
To match the Grandmama –
Staid sleeping – there –

Day – rattles – too
Stealth's – slow –
The Sun has got as far
As the third Sycamore –
rooster Screams Chanticleer
'Who's there?'

73

And Echoes – Trains away,
Sneer – 'Where'!
While the old Couple, just astir,
Fancy the Sunrise – left the door ajar!

EMILY DICKINSON

The Wind begun to rock the Grass

The Wind begun to rock the Grass
With threatening Tunes and low –
He threw a Menace at the Earth –
A Menace at the Sky.

The Leaves unhooked themselves from Trees –
And started all abroad
The Dust did scoop itself like Hands
And threw away the Road.

The Wagons quickened on the Streets
The Thunder hurried slow –
The Lightning showed a Yellow Beak
And then a livid Claw.

The Birds put up the Bars to Nests –
The Cattle fled to Barns –
There came one drop of Giant Rain
And then as if the Hands

That held the Dams had parted hold
The Waters Wrecked the Sky,
But overlooked my Father's House –
Just quartering a Tree –

EMILY DICKINSON

Sonnet 72

Hallowe'en. She dressed up in a sheet,
A paper crown, a tail, a fierce expression,
High-button shoes, not fitting, on her feet,
A broken mask, her proudest child-possession,
A lantern on the handle of a broom,
While over the sky of her anticipation,
Shining and far away though in that room,
Feet, lantern, hands leapt like a constellation.
Outdoors she waved her lantern in wild daring
And yelled at a stranger passing in the night,
Half to cheer herself and half in play.
But scared herself with her own sudden scaring,
And ran from what she thought would run away,
And found she could not even frighten fright.

PAUL ENGLE

The Devil

What I'm going to tell you
is strictly on the level:
I have seen the Devil.

The Devil sleeps but doesn't snore,
he blows into his beard.
The Devil never smiles,
his thirteen teeth are weird.
The Devil's all alone,
he shakes because he's scared.
The Devil seems unhappy,
his beard drips with tears.

The Devil's in my closet.
If my closet had a door
I'd slam it on his beard.

RICHARD J. MARGOLIS

Ladles and Jellyspoons

Ladles and jellyspoons:
I come before you
To stand behind you
And tell you something
I know nothing about.

Next Thursday,
The day after Friday,
There'll be a ladies' meeting
For men only.

Wear your best clothes
If you haven't any,
And if you can come
Please stay home.

Admission is free,
You can pay at the door.
We'll give you a seat
So you can sit on the floor.

It makes no difference
Where you sit;
The kid in the gallery
Is sure to spit.

TRADITIONAL ENGLISH

The Story of a Story

Once upon a time there was a story

Its end came
Before its beginning
And its beginning came
After its end

Its heroes entered it
After their death
And left it
Before their birth

Its heroes talked
About some earth about some heaven
They said all sorts of things

Only they didn't say
What they themselves didn't know
That they are only heroes in a story

In a story whose end comes
Before its beginning
And whose beginning comes
After its end

VASKO POPA
Yugoslavian poem translated from the Serbo-Croatian by Anne Pennington

The Sea Battle

An American aircraft carrier
and a Gothic cathedral
simultaneously sank each other
in the middle of the Pacific.
To the last
the young curate played on the organ.
Now aeroplanes and angels hang in the air
and have nowhere to land.

GÜNTER GRASS German poem translated by Michael Hamburger

Korf's Joke

Korf invents a novel kind of joke
which won't take effect for many hours.
Everyone is bored when first he hears it.

But he will, as though a fuse were burning,
suddenly wake up in bed at night time,
smiling sweetly like a well-fed baby.

CHRISTIAN MORGENSTERN German poem translated by Max Knight

Middle Ages

I heard a clash, and a cry,
And a horseman fleeing the wood.
The moon hid in a cloud.
Deep in shadow I stood.
  'Ugly work!' thought I,
Holding my breath.
  'Men must be cruel and proud,
  Jousting for death.'

With gusty glimmering shone
The moon; and the wind blew colder.
A man went over the hill,
Bent to his horse's shoulder.
  'Time for me to be gone' . . .
Darkly I fled.
  Owls in the wood were shrill,
  And the moon sank red.

SIEGFRIED SASSOON

Narnian Suite

March for Strings, Kettledrums, and Sixty-Three Dwarfs

With plucking pizzicato and the prattle of the kettledrum
We're trotting into battle mid a clatter of accoutrement;
Our beards are big as periwigs and trickle with opopanax,
And trinketry and treasure twinkle out on every part of us –
    (Scrape! Tap! The fiddle and the kettledrum).

The chuckle-headed humans think we're only petty poppetry
And all our battle-tackle nothing more than pretty bric-à-brac;
But a little shrub has prickles, and they'll soon be in a pickle if
A scud of dwarfish archery has crippled all their cavalry –
    (Whizz! Twang! The quarrel and the javelin).

And when the tussle thickens we can writhe and wriggle under it;
Then dagger-point'll tickle 'em, and grab and grip'll grapple 'em,
And trap and trick'll trouble 'em and tackle 'em and topple 'em
Till they're huddled, all be-diddled, in the middle of our caper-
     ings —
        (Dodge! Jump! The wriggle and the summersault).

When we've scattered 'em and peppered 'em with pebbles from
     our catapults
We'll turn again in triumph and by crannies and by crevices
Go back to where the capitol and cradle of our people is,
Our forges and our furnaces, the caverns of the earth —
        (Gold! Fire! The anvil and the smithying).

March for Drum, Trumpet, and Twenty-One Giants

With stumping stride in pomp and pride
We come to thump and floor ye;
We'll bump your lumpish heads today
And tramp your ramparts into clay,
And as we stamp and romp and play
Our trump'll blow before us —
(crescendo) Oh tramp it, tramp it, tramp it, trumpet, trumpet blow before us!

We'll grind and break and bind and take
And plunder ye and pound ye!
With trundled rocks and bludgeon blow,
You dunderheads, we'll dint ye so
You'll blunder and run blind, as though
By thunder stunned, around us —
By thunder, thunder, thunder, thunder stunned around us!

Ho! tremble town and tumble down
And crumble shield and saber!
Your kings will mumble and look pale,
Your horses stumble or turn tail,
Your skimble-skamble counsels fail,
So rumble drum belabored —
(diminuendo) Oh rumble, rumble, rumble, rumble, rumble drum belabored!

C. S. LEWIS

Old War Song

The stones are all that last long.

TRADITIONAL
North American Indian poem translated from the Cheyenne by Frances Densmore

The Knight in Prison

Wearily, drearily,
Half the day long,
Flap the great banners
High over the stone;
Strangely and eerily
Sounds the wind's song,
Bending the banner poles.

While, all alone,
Watching the loophole's spark,
Lie I, with life all dark,
Feet tethered, hands fettered
Fast to the stone,
The grim walls square lettered
With prisoned men's groan.

Still strain the banner poles
Through the wind's song,
Westward the banner rolls
Over my wrong.

WILLIAM MORRIS

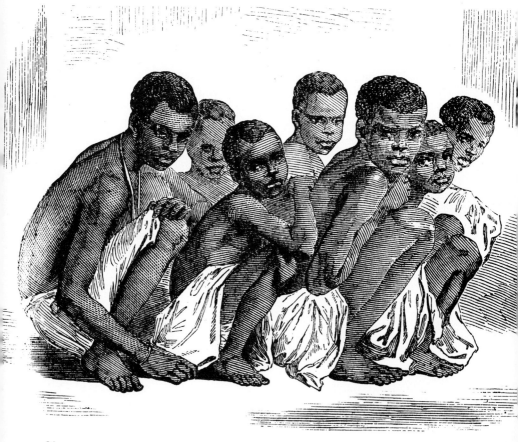

Song of the Galley Slaves

We pulled for you when the wind was against us and the
    sails were low.
    Will you never let us go?
We ate bread and onions when you took towns, or ran aboard
    quickly when you were beaten back by the foe.
The Captains walked up and down the deck in fair weather
    singing songs, but we were below.
We fainted with our chins on the oars and you did not see
    that we were idle, for we still swung to and fro.
    Will you never let us go?
The salt made the oar handles like shark skin; our knees
    were cut to the bone with salt cracks; our hair was stuck
    to our foreheads; and our lips were cut to the gums, and
    you whipped us because we could not row.
    Will you never let us go?
But, in a little time, we shall run out of the port holes as
    the water runs along the oar blade, and though you tell the
    others to row after us you will never catch us till you
    catch the oar-thresh and tie up the winds in the belly of
    the sail. Aho!
    Will you never let us go?

RUDYARD KIPLING

How Samson Bore Away the Gates of Gaza

A Negro Sermon

Once, in a night as black as ink,
She drove him out when he would not drink.
Round the house there were men in wait
Asleep in rows by the Gaza gate.
But the Holy Spirit was in this man.
Like a gentle wind he crept and ran.
('It is midnight,' said the big town clock.)

He lifted the gates up, post and lock.
The hole in the wall was high and wide
When he bore away old Gaza's pride
Into the deep of the night –
The bold Jack Johnson Israelite –
Samson –
The Judge,
The Nazarite.

The air was black, like the smoke of a dragon.
Samson's heart was as big as a wagon.
He sang like a shining golden fountain.
He sweated up to the top of the mountain.
He threw down the gates with a noise like judgement.
And the quails all ran with the big arousement.

But he wept – 'I must not love tough queens,
And spend on them my hard earned means.
I told that girl I would drink no more.
Therefore she drove me from her door.

Oh sorrow!
Sorrow!
I cannot hide.
Oh Lord look down from your chariot side.
You made me Judge, and I am not wise.
I am weak as a sheep for all my size.'

Let Samson
Be coming
Into your mind.

The moon shone out, the stars were gay.
He saw the foxes run and play.
He rent his garments, he rolled around
In deep repentance on the ground.

Then he felt a honey in his soul.
Grace abounding made him whole.
Then he saw the Lord in a chariot blue.
The gorgeous stallions whinnied and flew.
The iron wheels hummed an old hymn tune
And crunched in thunder over the moon.
And Samson shouted to the sky:

'My Lord, my Lord is riding high.'

Like a steed, he pawed the gates with his hoof.
He rattled the gates like rocks on the roof,
And danced in the night
On the mountain top,
Danced in the deep of the night:
The Judge, the holy Nazarite,
Whom ropes and chains could never bind.

Let Samson
Be coming
Into your mind.

Whirling his arms, like a top he sped.
His long black hair flew round his head
Like an outstretched net of silky cord,
Like a wheel of the chariot of the Lord.

Let Samson
Be coming
Into your mind.

Samson saw the sun anew.
He left the gates in the grass and dew.
He went to a county-seat a-nigh.
Found a harlot proud and high:
Philistine that no man could tame –
Delilah was her lady-name.
Oh sorrow,
Sorrow,
She was too wise.
She cut off his hair,
She put out his eyes.

Let Samson
Be coming
Into your mind.

VACHEL LINDSAY

Landscape with the Fall of Icarus

According to Brueghel
when Icarus fell
it was spring

a farmer was plowing
his field
the whole pageantry

of the year was
awake tingling
near

the edge of the sea

concerned
with itself

sweating in the sun
that melted
the wings' wax

insignificantly
off the coast
there was

a splash quite unnoticed
this was
Icarus drowning

WILLIAM CARLOS WILLIAMS

Child on Top of a Greenhouse

The wind billowing out the seat of my britches,
My feet crackling splinters of glass and dried putty,
The half-grown chrysanthemums staring up like accusers,
Up through the streaked glass, flashing with sunlight,
A few white clouds all rushing eastward,
A line of elms plunging and tossing like horses,
And everyone, everyone pointing up and shouting!

THEODORE ROETHKE

Umbara's Song

Capsizing   me   striking   me
the wind blows   hard   the sea   long stretched
between   striking   hard hitting   striking
me   dashing up   me   striking.

UMBARA Australian Aborigine poem translated by A.W. Howitt

As when a man

As when a man, that sails in a balloon,
  Downlooking sees the solid shining ground
Stream from beneath him in the broad blue noon,
  Tilth, hamlet, mead and mound:

And takes his flags and waves them to the mob,
  That shout below, all faces turned to where
Glows rubylike the far-up crimson globe,
  Filled with a finer air . . .

ALFRED, LORD TENNYSON

pattern of plowing

90

Turkey in the Straw

As I was a-gwine on down the road,
With a tired team and a heavy load,
I cracked my whip and the leader sprung,
I says day-day to the wagon tongue.

> Turkey in the straw, haw, haw, haw,
> Turkey in the hay, hay, hay, hay,
> Roll 'em up and twist 'em up – a high tuck a-haw,
> And hit 'em up a tune called *Turkey in the Straw*.

So I went a rackin' on down the road,
I met Miss Terrapin and Mister Toad,
And every time that toad would jump,
Miss Terrapin hide behind the stump.

I met an old catfish swimmin' in the stream,
I axed that old catfish what do he mean,
Grabbed that catfish right by the snout
And turnt Mister Catfish wrongside out.

I loves to go a-fishin' on a bright summer day,
To see the perches and the catfish play,
With their hands in their pockets and their pockets in their
    pants
Would you like to see the ladies do the kootchie-kootchie
    dance?

TRADITIONAL AMERICAN

The Fence

There was a fence with spaces you
Could look through if you wanted to.

An architect who saw this thing
Stood there one summer evening,

Took out the spaces with great care
And built a castle in the air.

The fence was utterly dumbfounded:
Each post stood there with nothing round it.

A sight most terrible to see.
(They charged it with indecency.)

The architect then ran away
To Afric- or Americ-ay.

CHRISTIAN MORGENSTERN German poem translated by R.F.C. Hull

Greer County

How happy am I when I crawl into bed –
A rattlesnake hisses a tune at my head,
A gay little centipede, all without fear,
Crawls over my pillow and into my ear.

My clothes is all ragged as my language is rough,
My bread is corn-dodgers, both solid and tough;
But yet I am happy, and live at my ease
On sorghum molasses, bacon, and cheese.

cake of cornbread

Good-bye to Greer County where blizzards arise,
Where the sun never sinks and a flea never dies,
And the wind never ceases but always remains
Till it starves us to death on our government claims.

Farewell to Greer County, farewell to the West,
I'll travel back East to the girl I love best,
I'll travel back to Texas and marry me a wife,
And quit cornbread for the rest of my life.

TRADITIONAL AMERICAN

The Stockman's Last Bed

Whether Stockman or not, for one moment give ear,
Poor Jack's breathed his last, and no more shall we hear
The crack of his whip, or his nag's lively trot,
His clear 'Go ahead', or his jingling quart pot.

> For they've laid him where wattles
>   Their sweet perfume shed,
> And tall gum trees shadow
>   The Stockman's last bed.

herding While drafting some cattle, down came his good horse,
'At last,' cried poor Jack, 'I have run my last course,
I will never more sit in the saddle again,
Or bound like a kangaroo over the plain.'

Then, Stockmen, if ever at some future day,
In search of a mob you should happen to stray,
And come to the spot where poor Jack's bones are laid,
Far, far from the home where in childhood he played

> Tread lightly, where wattles
>   Their sweet perfume shed,
> And tall gum trees shadow
>   The Stockman's last bed.

TRADITIONAL AUSTRALIAN

Joshua Fit de Battle of Jericho

Joshua fit de battle of Jericho,
Jericho, Jericho,
Joshua fit de battle of Jericho,
And de walls come tumbling down.

You may talk about your king of Gideon,
Talk about your man of Saul,
Dere's none like good old Joshua
At de battle of Jericho.

Up to de walls of Jericho
He marched with spear in hand;
'Go blow them ram horns,' Joshua cried,
''Cause the battle am in my hand.'

Then de lamb ram sheep horns begin to blow,
Trumpets begin to sound,
Joshua commanded de children to shout,
And de walls come tumbling down.
                    (That morning.)

Joshua fit de battle of Jericho,
Jericho, Jericho,
Joshua fit de battle of Jericho,
And de walls come tumbling down.

TRADITIONAL AMERICAN

Thunder and Lightning

Blood punches through every vein
As lightning strips the windowpane.

Under its flashing whip, a white
Village leaps to light.

On tubs of thunder, fists of rain
Slog it out of sight again.

Blood punches the heart with fright
As rain belts the village night.

JAMES KIRKUP

Storms

My mum hates thunder
She plugs her ears with a towel
And lies on the settee
As though someone were coming to get her.

But me, I'm alright
I don't mind a bit
I'm a bit edgy about lightning
But thunder doesn't bother me at all.

GLYNIS BURR

Mud Time: Southern Indiana

The playground is red mud.

I labor on clay feet.

A whole week of cold April rain
has swum all the feathery leaves.

I see my face in a puddle.
In the water I am crying.

My raincoat smells like fish.

My hat has caught a creek.

Miss Wing, the town librarian,
sloshes by, girgling behind gold teeth.

The bell rings. The schoolhouse
sails away on a book of clouds.

DAVE ETTER

The Fog

I saw the fog grow thick,
sight   Which soon made blind my ken;
It made tall men of boys,
   And giants of tall men.

It clutched my throat, I coughed;
   Nothing was in my head
Except two heavy eyes
   Like balls of burning lead.

And when it grew so black
   That I could know no place,
I lost all judgment then,
   Of distance and of space.

The street lamps, and the lights
   Upon the halted cars,
Could either be on earth
   Or be the heavenly stars.

A man passed by me close,
   I asked my way, he said,
'Come, follow me, my friend' –
   I followed where he led.

He rapped the stones in front,
   'Trust me,' he said, 'and come';
I followed like a child –
   A blind man led me home.

W.H. DAVIES

From the fog

From the fog a gull flies slowly
and is lost in fog. The buildings are only clouds.

CHARLES REZNIKOFF

The Coming of the Cold

The ribs of leaves lie in the dust,
The beak of frost has picked the bough,
The briar bears its thorn, and drought
Has left its ravage on the field.
The season's wreckage lies about,
Late autumn fruit is rotted now.
All shade is lean, the antic branch
Jerks skyward at the touch of wind,
Dense trees no longer hold the light,
The hedge and orchard grove are thinned.
The dank bark dries beneath the sun,
The last of harvesting is done.
All things are brought to barn and fold.
The oak leaves strain to be unbound,
The sky turns dark, the year grows old,
The buds draw in before the cold.

THEODORE ROETHKE

Northern Spring

1   Surrounded by gamy dogs
and flowers with strange names,
the elm tree stump
grows a head of grizzly hair.

2   There are piney smells in the fog.
There are shiny windows in the sky.
There are tiny veins in the leaves.

3   Beyond the cat, lean sparrows
explode in a hedge of sticks.

4   The junkman bells his brown horse.

DAVE ETTER

The Computer's First Christmas Card

```
jollymerry
hollyberry
jollyberry
merryholly
happyjolly
jollyjelly
jellybelly
bellymerry
hollyheppy
jollyMolly
marryJerry
merryHarry
hoppyBarry
heppyJarry
boppyheppy
berryjorry
jorryjolly
moppyjelly
Mollymerry
Jerryjolly
bellyboppy
jorryhoppy
hollymoppy
Barrymerry
Jarryhappy
happyboppy
boppyjolly
jollymerry
merrymerry
merrymerry
merryChris
ammerryasa
Chrismerry
asMERRYCHR
YSANTHEMUM
```

EDWIN MORGAN

Excelsior

Who has gone farthest? for I would go farther,
And who has been just? for I would be the most just person
of the earth,
And who most cautious? for I would be more cautious,
And who has been happiest? O I think it is I – I think no
one was ever happier than I,
And who has lavish'd all? for I lavish constantly the best
I have,
And who proudest? for I think I have reason to be the
proudest son alive – for I am the son of the brawny and
tall-topt city,
And who has been bold and true? for I would be the boldest
and truest being of the universe,
And who benevolent? for I would show more benevolence
than all the rest,
And who has receiv'd the love of the most friends? for I know
what it is to receive the passionate love of many friends,
And who possesses a perfect and enamor'd body? for I do
not believe any one possesses a more perfect or enamor'd
body than mine,
And who thinks the amplest thoughts? for I would surround
those thoughts,
And who has made hymns fit for the earth? for I am mad
with devouring ecstasy to make joyous hymns for the
whole earth.

WALT WHITMAN

Answers to Riddles

Six Riddles page 2

1 The wall will neither break nor fall
2 Anne
3 The eye of deceit
  Can best counterfeit
  And so, I suppose,
  Can best count 'er toes.
4 A watermelon
5 A needle and thread
6 C A T
  H A Y
  I C E
  Y O U

Decapitations page 4

Whoop   Brook   Trout   Spear
March   Blast   Spain

Natural Song (Riddle) page 28

Tree

Tunes for Some Poems

Turkey in the Straw

As— I was a—gwine on— down the road, With a

ti- red team and a heav- y load, I—

cracked my— whip— and the lea-der sprung, I—

chorus

says day-day —— to the wa- gon tongue. Tur-key in the straw,

haw, haw, haw, Tur-key in the hay, hay, hay, hay,

Roll 'em up and twist 'em up a high tuck a-haw, And —

hit 'em up a tune called *Tur-key in the Straw.*

Greer County

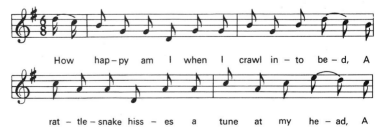

How hap-py am I when I crawl in-to be-d, A

rat-tle-snake hiss-es a tune at my he-ad, A

105

gay lit-tle cen-ti-pede, all with-out fe-ar, Crawls

ov-er my pil-low and in-to my ear.

The Stockman's Last Bed

Wheth-er Stock-man or not, for one mom-ent give ear, Poor

Jack's breathed his last, and no more shall we hear The— crack of his

whip, or his nag's live-ly trot, His clear 'Go a-head', or his

chorus

jing-ling quart pot. For they've laid him where wat-tles Their sweet per-fume

shed, And— tall gum-trees sha-dow And tall gum-trees sha-dow, And—

tall gum-trees shad-ow The Stock-man's last bed.

Joshua Fit de Battle of Jericho

Josh-ua fit de bat-tle of— Jer-i-cho—,

Jer-i-cho—, Jer-i-cho—, Josh-ua fit de bat-tle of—

Jer- i- cho, And de walls come tum-bling down. You may

talk a-bout your king of Gi- de- on, You may

talk a-bout your man of Saul, Dere's none like good old Josh-ua At de

bat- tle of Jer- i- cho. Up to de walls of Jer- i- cho, He

marched with spear in hand; 'Go blow them ram horns,'

Josh- u- a cried, "Cause the bat- tle am in my hand.'

Josh-ua fit de bat- tle of— Jer- i- cho—,

Jer- i- cho—, Jer- i- cho—, Josh-ua fit de bat- tle of —

fine

Jer- i- cho, And de walls come tum- bling down.

Then de lamb ram sheep horns be- gin to blow, Trum-pets be-gin to

107

sound, Josh- u- a com-mand-ed the child-ren to shout, And de

walls come tum-bling down.

d.s. al fine

Acknowledgements

For permission to use copyright material acknowledgement is made to the following:

Poetry For 'We are going to see the rabbit' by Alan Brownjohn to Macmillan & Co. Ltd; for the extract from *Briggflats* by Basil Bunting to the author and Fulcrum Press; for 'Storms' by Glynis Burr to the author; for 'Decapitations' by 'C. C.' as arranged by George Hitchcock to Kayak; for 'Young Shepherd Bathing his Feet' by Peter Clarke from *Poems from Black Africa* edited by Langston Hughes to the Indiana University Press; for 'The Frog' from *Collected Poems* by W. H. Davies to Mrs H. M. Davies, Jonathan Cape Ltd and the Wesleyan University Press; for 'The government said' by Julie Dewberry to the author and *Living Language*, BBC Schools Radio; for 'Sonnet 72' by Paul Engle to the author; for 'Mud Time: Southern Indiana' and 'Northern Spring' from *Last Train to Prophetstown* by Dave Etter to the University of Nebraska Press; for 'The Song of the Bottle' translated by A. Fiedler from *The Unwritten Song* edited by Willard R. Trask to the Macmillan Company of New York; for 'The Sea Battle' from *Selected Poems* by Günter Grass translated by Michael Hamburger to Secker & Warburg Ltd and Harcourt, Brace & World Inc.; for 'The Legs' from *Collected Poems 1965* by Robert Graves to the author and Collins-Knowlton-Wing Inc.; for 'Orange and golden' and 'With your fists ablaze' from *Hawkweed* by Paul Goodman to Random House Inc.; for 'A bitter morning', 'Flashing neon night' and 'Rain drums on the pane' by J. W. Hackett to Japan Publications Inc.; for 'The Big Nasturtiums' by Robert Beverley Hale to the New Yorker Magazine Inc.; for 'Uncle Jack and the Other Man' by Keith Harrison to the author; for 'The Annunciation' by Miroslav Holub translated by George Theiner from *New Writing from Czechoslovakia* edited by George Theiner to Penguin Books Ltd; for 'Fairy Tale' from *Selected Poems* by Miroslav Holub translated by Ian Milner to Penguin Books Ltd; for 'Sometimes when I talk' by Jane Horvitz from *Young Voices* edited by L. Schaefer and H. Mellor to the Bruce Publishing Company; for 'Still Here' from *Selected Poems* by Langston Hughes to Alfred Knopf Inc.; for 'Moon-Hops' from *The Earth Owl* by Ted Hughes to Faber & Faber Ltd; for 'The Garden Hose' by Beatrice Janosco to the author; for 'Song of the Galley-Slaves' an extract from 'The Finest Story in the World' from *Many Inventions* by Rudyard Kipling to Mrs George Bambridge, Macmillan & Co. Ltd and Doubleday & Co. Inc.; for 'Thunder and Lightning' from *The Prodigal Son* by James Kirkup to the author; for 'The Dead Butterfly' from *With Eyes at the Back of our Heads* by Denise Levertov to New Directions Publishing Corporation; for 'The Sharks' by Denise Levertov to the author; for 'Narnian Suite' from *Poems* by C. S. Lewis to Harcourt Brace Jovanovich, Inc.; for 'Sink Song' by J. A. Lindon from *The Book of Comic and Curious Verse* to Penguin Books Ltd; for 'How Samson Bore Away the Gates of Gaza' and 'The Sea Serpent Chantey' from *Selected Poems* by Vachel Lindsay to the Macmillan Company of New York; for 'The Devil' from *Looking for a Place* by Richard J. Margolis to J. B. Lippincott Company; for 'The Computer's First Christmas Card', 'French Persian Cats Having a Ball', 'Orgy' and 'A View of Things' from *The Second Life* by Edwin of California Press; for 'The Knight in Prison' by William Morris to the author; for 'Starry Snail', 'The Story of a Story' and 'The Yawn of Yawns' from *Selected Poems* by Vasko Popa translated by Anne Pennington to Penguin Books Ltd; for 'Bug Words', 'Sounds' and 'Squishy Words' from *Ounce, Dice, Trice* by Alastair

Morgan to the Edinburgh University Press; for 'The Experiment' and 'The Fence' translated by R. F. C. Hull and 'Korf's Joke' and 'The Snail's Monologue' translated by Max Knight from *Gallows Songs* by Christian Morgenstern to the University Reid to J. M. Dent & Sons Ltd and Atlantic-Little, Brown & Co.; for 'About an excavation', 'Among the heaps', 'From the fog', 'The house-wreckers', 'Permit me to warn you', 'Suburb' and 'This smoky winter morning' from *By the Waters of Manhattan* by Charles Reznikoff to New Directions Publishing Corporation; for 'The Bat', 'Child on Top of a Greenhouse', 'The Coming of the Cold', 'Mips and ma the mooly moo', 'Running lightly over spongy ground' from 'The Lost Son' and 'The way to the boiler was dark' from 'The Return' from *Collected Poems* by Theodore Roethke to Faber & Faber Ltd and Doubleday & Co. Inc.; for 'Hard Cheese' by Justin St John to the author; for 'Arithmetic' and 'Remember the chameleon' from *Collected Poems* by Carl Sandburg, 'Elephants are Different to Different People' from *Home Front Memo* by Carl Sandburg, 'The concrete highways' from *Good Morning, America* by Carl Sandburg, and 'I don't know where I'm going' and 'What kind of a liar are you?' from *The People, Yes* by Carl Sandburg to Harcourt, Brace & World Inc.; for 'Middle Ages' by Siegfried Sassoon to G. T. Sassoon; for 'The Toaster' from *Laughing Time* by William Jay Smith to Faber & Faber Ltd and Atlantic-Little, Brown & Co.; for 'The Apple Tree' and 'Behind the Hill' from *Collected Poems* by James Stephens to Macmillan & Co. Ltd, the Macmillan Company of Canada Ltd and the Macmillan Company of New York; for 'Earthy Anecdote' from *Selected Poems* by Wallace Stevens to Faber & Faber Ltd and Alfred Knopf Inc.; for 'Natural Song' from *To Mix with Time* by May Swenson to the author and Charles Scribner's Sons; for 'accidentally' and 'just felt like it' from *Poems to Eat* by Ishikawa Takuboku to Kodensha International Ltd; for 'What's inside the moon?' by Vivian Tuft and Fontessa Moore from *Wishes, Lies and Dreams* by Kenneth Koch to Random House, Inc.; for 'Dunce Song No. 4' and 'Indomitable' from *New and Collected Poems 1924–1963* by Mark van Doren to the author and Hill & Wang Inc.; for 'Upstairs' by John Stevens Wade to the author; for 'Horses' by Lynne Williams to the author; for 'Landscape with the Fall of Icarus' from *Pictures from Brueghel* by William Carlos Williams to MacGibbon & Kee Ltd and New Directions Publishing Corporation; for 'On Making Tea' by R. L. Wilson from *Scottish Poetry 1* to the Edinburgh University Press; for 'Kingley Bottom' from *Collected Poems* by Andrew Young to Rupert Hart-Davis Ltd; for 'A Withered Tree' by Han Yü translated by A. C. Graham from *Poems of the Late T'ang* to Penguin Books Ltd.

List of Illustrations

Index of Titles and First Lines

114

Index of Poets, Translators and Collectors